◁ **W9-AVD-178**

Authentic Victorian Stencil Designs

EDITED BY

Carol Belanger Grafton

DOVER PUBLICATIONS, INC.
NEW YORK

PUBLISHER'S NOTE

This sourcebook of authentic period designs brings together 124 striking stencil patterns that first appeared in the late nineteenth-century periodical *Deutsches Maler-Journal.* Its contents complement, but do not duplicate, those of Edmund V. Gillon, Jr.'s *Victorian Stencils for Design and Decoration* (Dover 0-486-21995-X, published 1968).

The anonymous creators of this decorative material adapted the exuberance of Victorian ornament to the technical requirements of stencil painting, giving the elaborate work remarkable boldness and vigor. The same designs that adorned the homes and public buildings of Victoria's time can now find new use in textile, wallpaper and tile design, or, further afield, in a wide range of commercial art applications.

Noted graphic designer Carol Belanger Grafton has selected many of the most interesting of these heretofore inaccessible motifs and arranged them for ready use and appreciation by artists, craftsmen and decorators.

Copyright © 1982 by Dover Publications, Inc.
All rights reserved under Pan American and International Copyright Conventions.

Published in Canada by General Publishing Company, Ltd., 30 Lesmill Road, Don Mills, Toronto, Ontario.

Published in the United Kingdom by Constable and Company, Ltd., 3 The Lanchesters, 162-164 Fulham Palace Road, London W6 9ER.

Authentic Victorian Stencil Designs is a new work, first published by Dover Publications, Inc., in 1982.

DOVER *Pictorial Archive* SERIES

This book belongs to the Dover Pictorial Archive Series. You may use the designs and illustrations for graphics and crafts applications, free and without special permission, provided that you include no more than ten in the same publication or project. (For permission for additional use, please write to: Permissions Department, Dover Publications, Inc., 180 Varick Street, New York, N.Y. 10014.)

However, republication or reproduction of any illustration by any other graphic service, whether it be in a book or in any other design resource, is strictly prohibited.

Library of Congress Cataloging-in-Publication Data

Main entry under title:

Authentic Victorian stencil designs.

(Dover pictorial archive series)
"First appeared in the late nineteenth-century Deutsches Maler-Journal"—Publisher's note.
1. Stencil work—History—19th century. 2. Decoration and ornament—Victorian style. I. Grafton, Carol Belanger.
NK8650.A9 1982   745.7'3   82-9410
ISBN 0-486-24337-0   AACR2

Manufactured in the United States of America
Dover Publications, Inc.
31 East 2nd Street
Mineola, N.Y. 11501

1

2

3

4

5

8

10

13

14

15

17

18

19

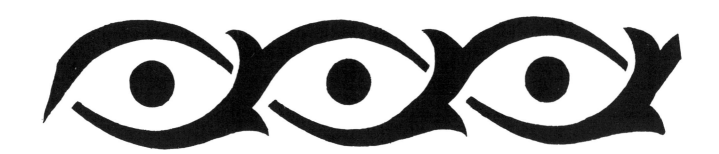

27

29

31

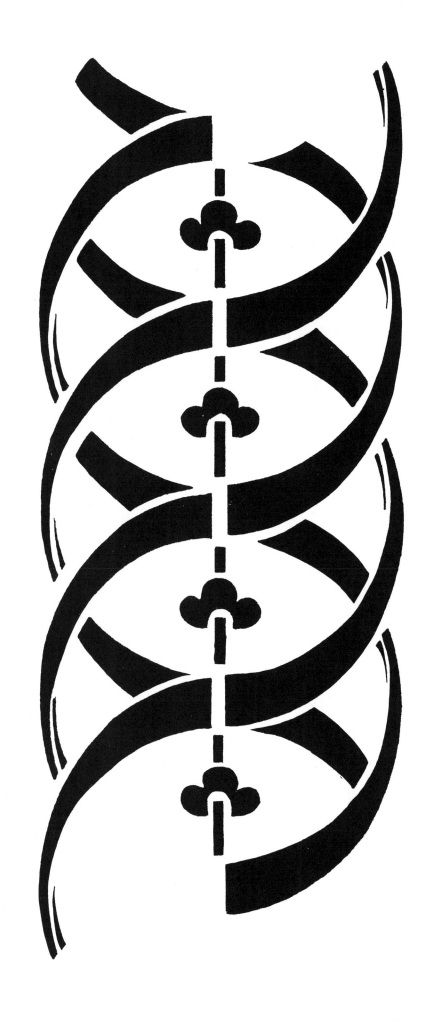

34

40

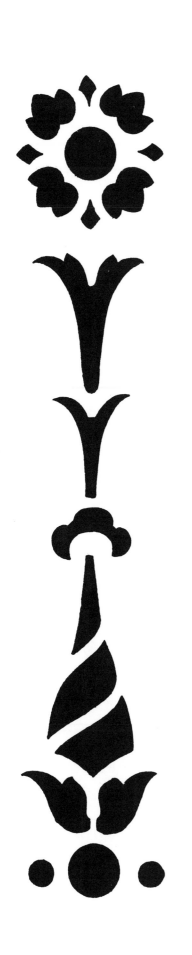

41

43

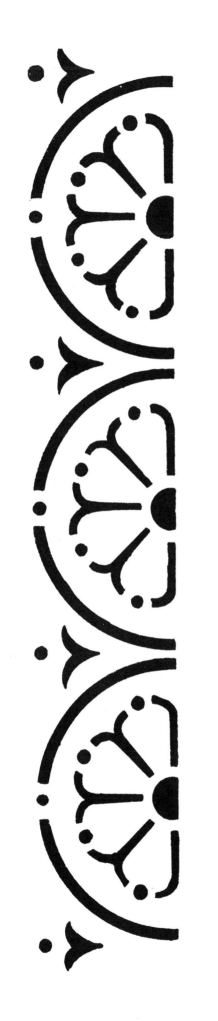

46

47

49

51

54